FISHING SKILLS

Fly Tying

Tony Whieldon

Introduction by Russ Symons

WARD LOCK

© Ward Lock Limited 1986

First published in Great Britain in 1986
by Ward Lock Limited, Artillery House,
Artillery Row, London SW1P 1RT,
a Cassell Company

Reprinted 1988, 1989

Printed and bound in the UK by The Bath Press

British Library Cataloguing in Publication Data

Whieldon, Tony
    Fly tying.———(Fishing skills)
    1. Fly tying   2. Trout fishing
    I. Title   II. Series
    688.7′912   SH451

ISBN 0-7063-6447-3

Contents

Introduction

I am constantly amazed by the fact that such noble fish as the trout and salmon can be caught on the unlikely creations of fur and feather that we fishermen cobble together and call a fly – whether it be an imitation of some natural insect, or a flashy fly that arouses the fish's predatory instinct. Such is the enjoyment found in tying and fishing the fly that often the angler becomes as firmly hooked on the sport as the fish on the fly.

True success as an angler cannot be bought, and this applies in particular to the business of becoming a successful fly fisherman. The most expensive and perfect fly rod in the whole world cannot cover up deficiencies in a person's casting technique. A wallet of the most perfectly tied flies will assure some degree of success, if properly fished, but most fly patterns will have a regional or seasonal variation, often of a most subtle kind.

Such variations are the result of evolution, and by an intelligent response to conditions peculiar to a particular fishery or environment. The only way the fisherman can obtain flies that are in perfect accord with both his own observations of these variations, and his subjective preferences, is to tie them himself.

Tony Whieldon has drawn this book almost, it could be said, from the heart. His first love is of flyfishing, and his strongly-held view that no one can consider himself/herself a flyfisher until an apprenticeship at a fly-tying vice has been served, shines from every page.

It is through his artist's eye and interpretation – his observation of detail and the almost simplistic representation of insect life which he creates at his vice – that his skill at recognizing those features which a fish expects to occur in nature, becomes obvious. This is one of the more obtuse skills of an angler, but an essential one to any who would aspire to success.

There are some who believe in the exact imitation, or as close to it as possible within the conventions of fly fishing. Their insect imitations are wonderously close to the real thing and are a marvellous demonstration of the fly-tyer's art and skill.

But there has always been another argument. All too often the water is cloudy; water has an inherent optical distortion; light and shadow and the time of day affect the appearance of objects in the water: therefore, in view of nature's infinite nuances, the exact imitation is not always the best fish-catcher.

Tony's argument is that rather than let these nuances of light and shadow defeat the object, they should be used to enhance the allure of the fly. The silhouette should be right, but not sharply defined. Where there is a shiny surface in nature, use a material which will reflect or sparkle. Colours should be representative rather than faithfully duplicated, especially as different materials may not transmit the same colour as the original (one reason, incidentally, to follow a traditional pattern material that has been found to work).

Most important of all, however – the fly should be fished in the right manner, in the right place, and at the right time. This feel for what is right – almost an extra-sensory perception possessed by some anglers as to where the fish will be and what they will be feeding on – is a perception developed through being prepared to listen to what others have to say, and through observation and an understanding of the living world around us.

This sense of accord and observation is far more important than the precise execution of a fly-tying recipe. However, natural proportion, symmetry and movement should exert their influence not only in the tying of the fly, but in its presentation to the fish.

Tony's skill as a flyfisherman is matched by his artistic ability, then blended with a round mixture of common sense and practical ability, so that this little book contains all that is really necessary to tie flies which are effective fish-catchers. Beyond this book practice will make perfect – or so we like to think.

Russell Symons,
Plymouth, Devon.

April 1986

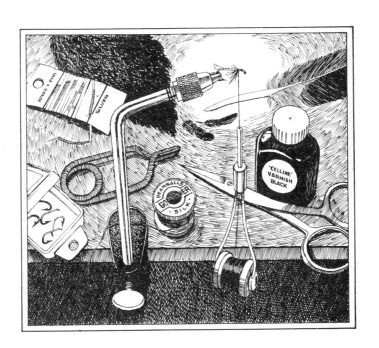

Tools

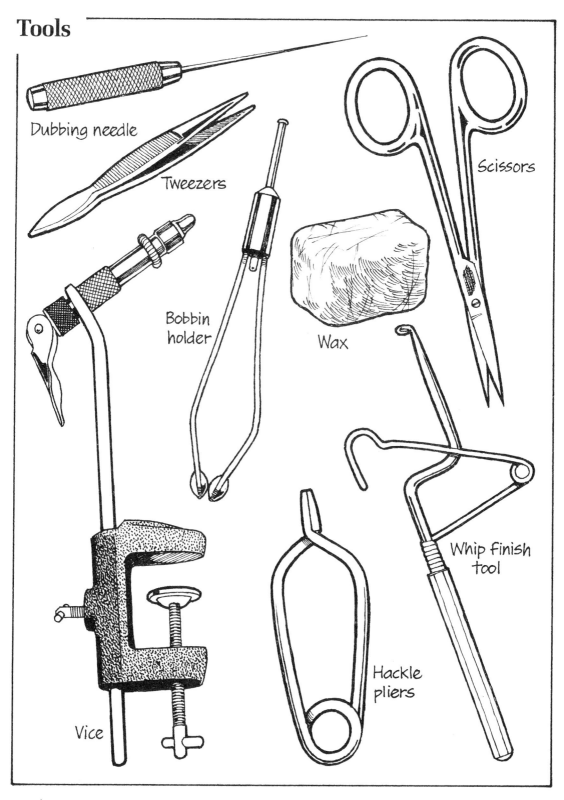

Dubbing needle

Tweezers

Scissors

Bobbin holder

Wax

Vice

Hackle pliers

Whip finish tool

Hooks

Sproat hooks with a turned-down eye are ideal for winged and hackled wet flies, and for certain short-bodied nymphs.

Fine wire hooks with a turned-up eye are best for dry flies.

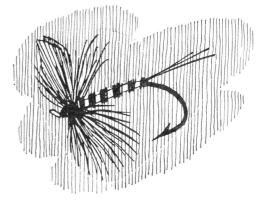

Long-shank hooks with a turned-down eye are used for dressing lures and nymphs.

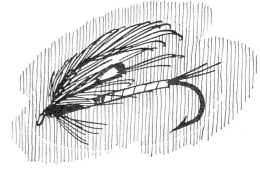

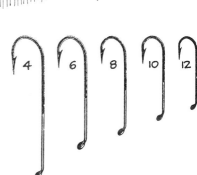

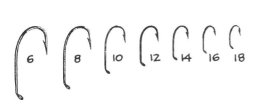

Materials

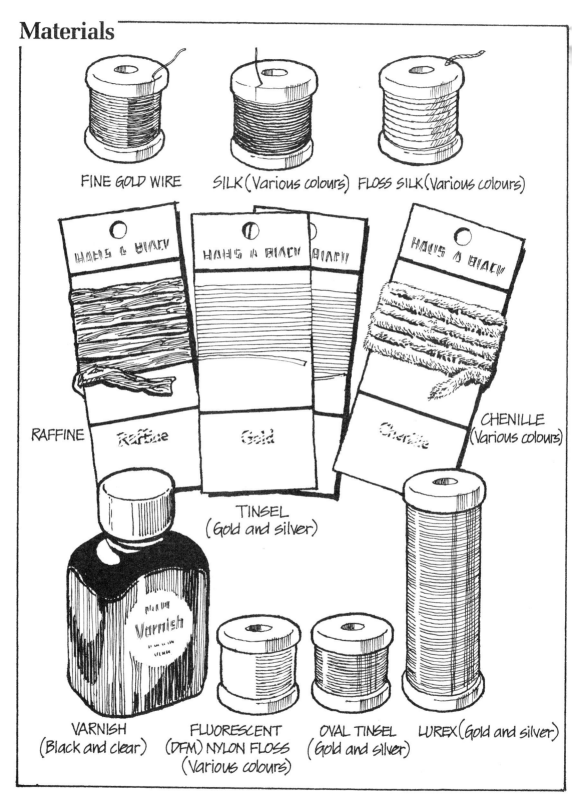

FINE GOLD WIRE

SILK (Various colours)

FLOSS SILK (Various colours)

RAFFINE

TINSEL
(Gold and silver)

CHENILLE
(Various colours)

VARNISH
(Black and clear)

FLUORESCENT
(DFM) NYLON FLOSS
(Various colours)

OVAL TINSEL
(Gold and silver)

LUREX (Gold and silver)

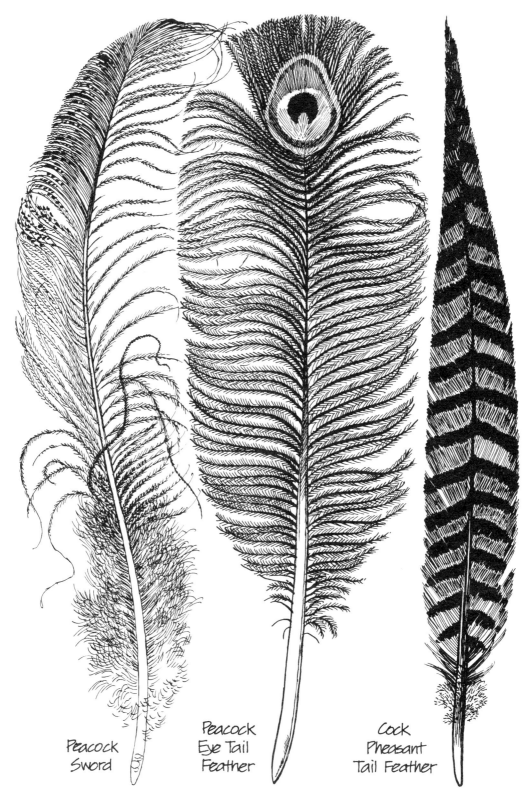

Peacock
Sword

Peacock
Eye Tail
Feather

Cock
Pheasant
Tail Feather

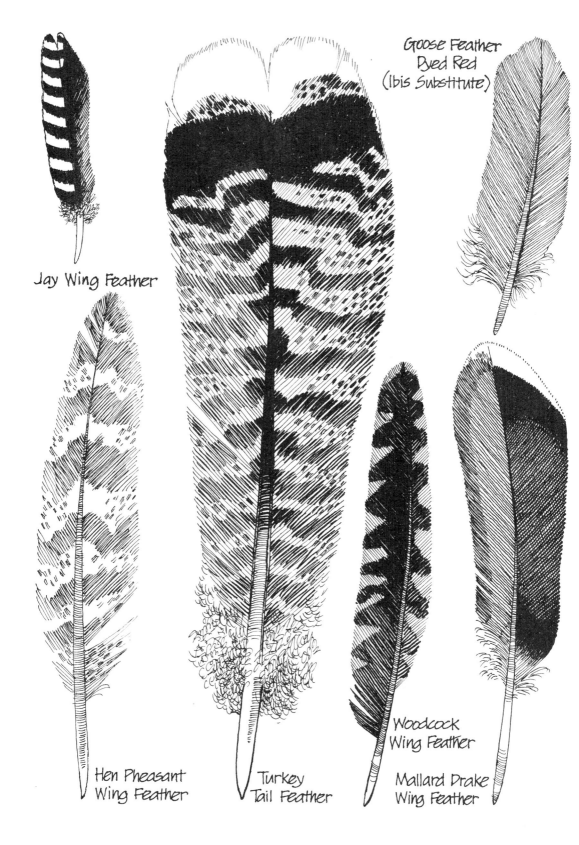

Jay Wing Feather

Goose Feather
Dyed Red
(Ibis Substitute)

Hen Pheasant
Wing Feather

Turkey
Tail Feather

Woodcock
Wing Feather

Mallard Drake
Wing Feather

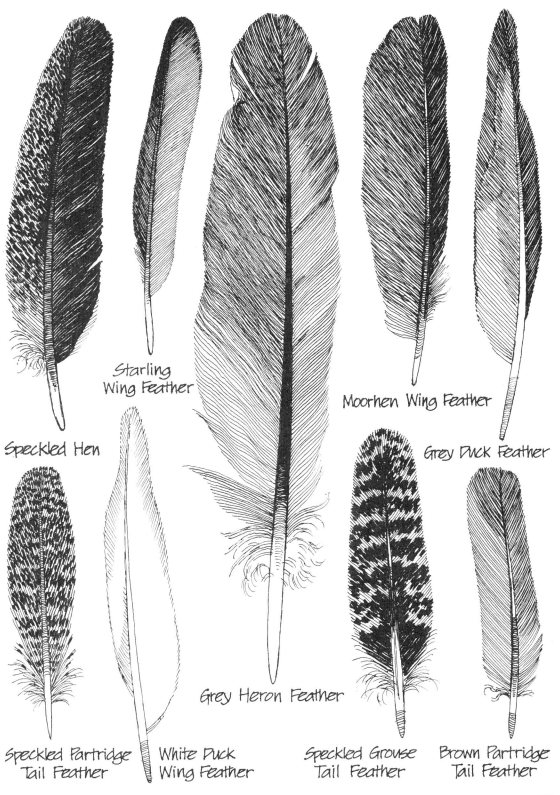

Starling
Wing Feather

Speckled Hen

Moorhen Wing Feather

Grey Duck Feather

Grey Heron Feather

Speckled Partridge
Tail Feather

White Duck
Wing Feather

Speckled Grouse
Tail Feather

Brown Partridge
Tail Feather

13

Cock hackles are best bought on the cape. The cape shown below is an actual size badger variation. The long-fibred hackles at the tip provide tail fibres for aquatic fly imitations and wings for lures (streamer flies). The middle region of the cape provides hackles for medium-size dry flies, while the small hackles at the base are ideal for dry flies tied to very small hooks. Saddle hackles, from the back of the cockerel, come individually and provide wings for large lures.

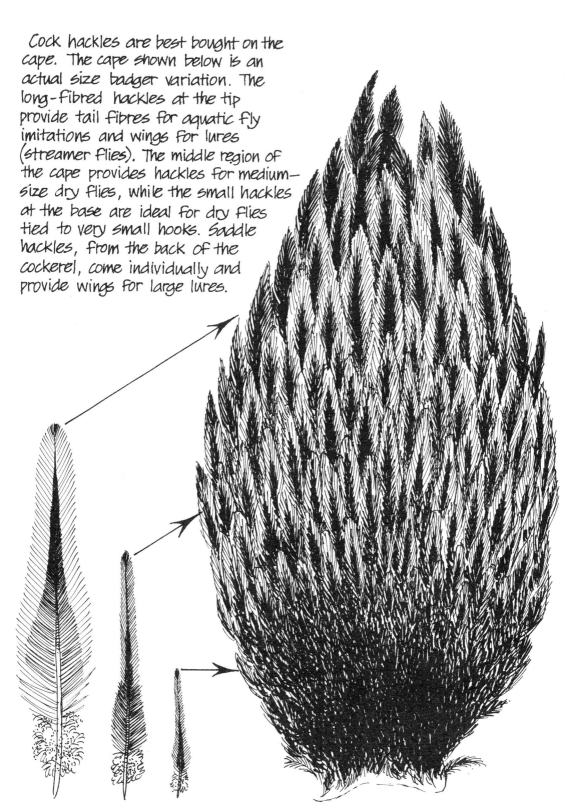

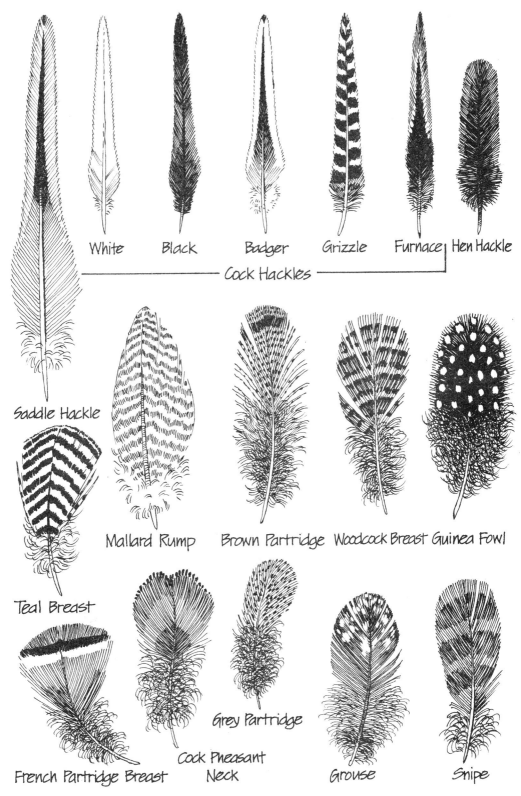

White   Black   Badger   Grizzle   Furnace   Hen Hackle

— Cock Hackles —

Saddle Hackle

Mallard Rump   Brown Partridge   Woodcock Breast   Guinea Fowl

Teal Breast

French Partridge Breast   Cock Pheasant Neck   Grey Partridge   Grouse   Snipe

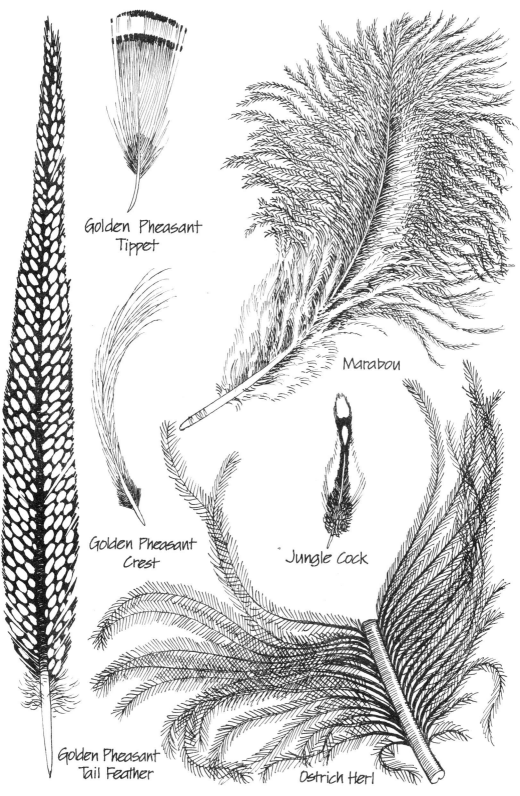

Golden Pheasant
Tippet

Marabou

Golden Pheasant
Crest

Jungle Cock

Golden Pheasant
Tail Feather

Ostrich Herl

Stoat Tail

Black Squirrel Tail   Grey Squirrel Tail   Hare's Ear

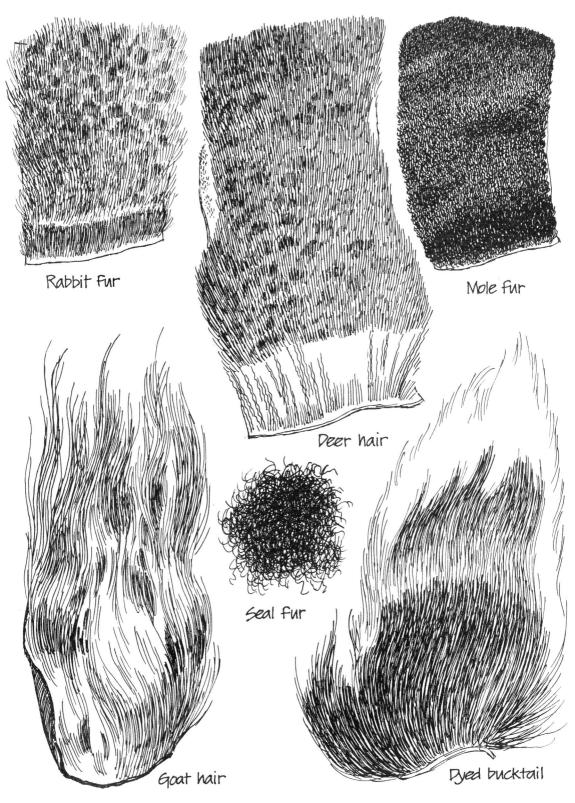

Rabbit fur

Mole fur

Deer hair

Goat hair

Seal fur

Dyed bucktail

18

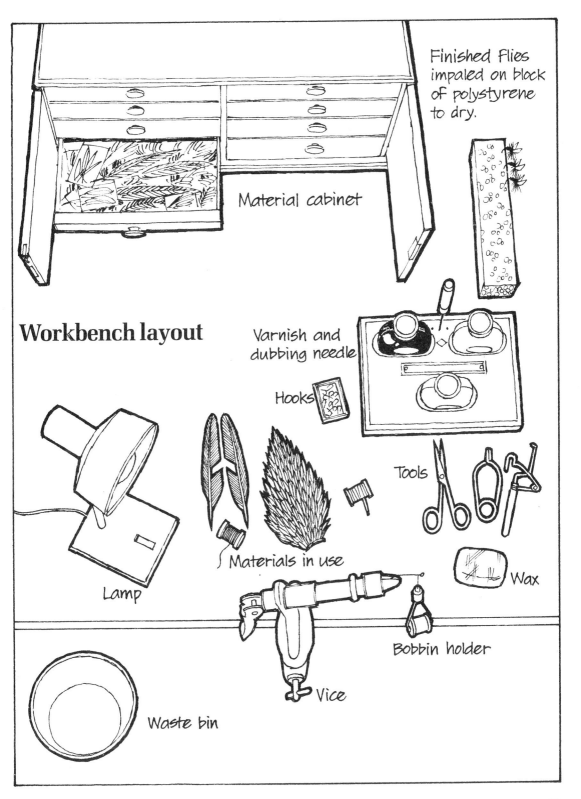

Finished flies
impaled on block
of polystyrene
to dry.

Material cabinet

Workbench layout

Varnish and
dubbing needle

Hooks

Tools

Lamp

Materials in use

Wax

Vice

Bobbin holder

Waste bin

EPHEMEROPTERA (Mayflies)

The trout's diet

Members of this group of insects all have upright wings and two or three tails. There are four stages in the metamorphosis: egg, nymph, sub-imago and imago. Fishermen refer to the sub-imago as the 'dun', and to the imago as the 'spinner'.

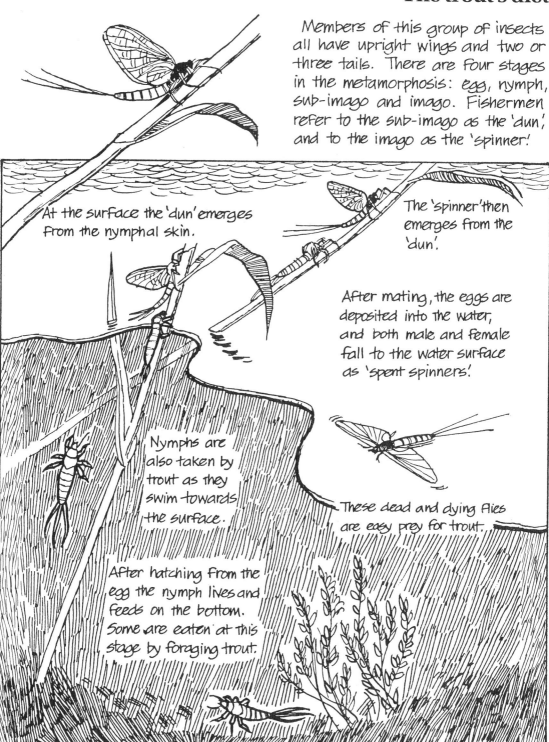

At the surface the 'dun' emerges from the nymphal skin.

The 'spinner' then emerges from the 'dun'.

After mating, the eggs are deposited into the water, and both male and female fall to the water surface as 'spent spinners'.

Nymphs are also taken by trout as they swim towards the surface.

These dead and dying flies are easy prey for trout.

After hatching from the egg the nymph lives and feeds on the bottom. Some are eaten at this stage by foraging trout.

Other groups of insects go through a similar sort of development as the Ephemeroptera. All the stages shown below form part of the trout's diet.

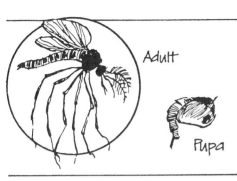

Adult

Pupa

DIPTERA: In this group, the midges (Chironomids) are of most interest to trout.

Larva

Larva (bloodworm)

TRICHOPTERA: This group includes the caddis or sedge flies.

Caddis larvae in cases

Pupa

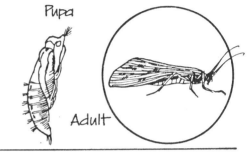

Adult

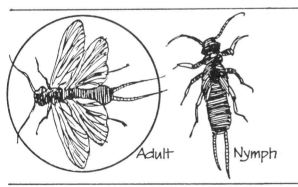

Adult

Nymph

PLECOPTERA: These are found mainly in stony rivers. The nymph of the large adult stonefly is very active, and is a main food item where it occurs.

ZYGOPTERA: Adult damselflies are occasionally taken by trout, but the nymph is a main food item.

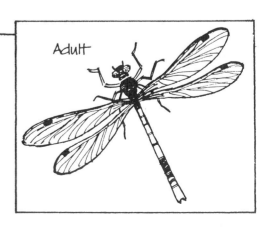

Adult

Nymph

Many other species of non-aquatic insects form part of the trout's diet. These are blown on to the surface of the water by the wind. Here are the two most commonly encountered.

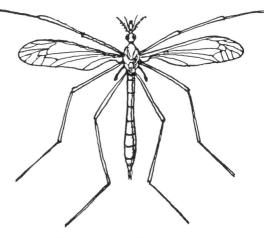

Hawthorn fly

Crane-fly or 'daddy-long-legs'.

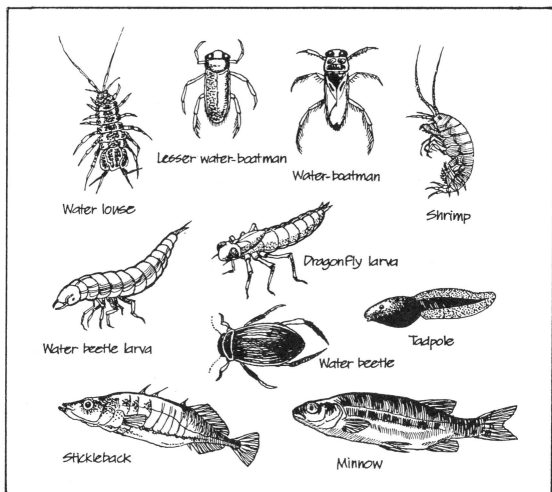

Water louse

Lesser water-boatman

Water-boatman

Shrimp

Water beetle larva

Dragonfly larva

Water beetle

Tadpole

Stickleback

Minnow

The artificial fly

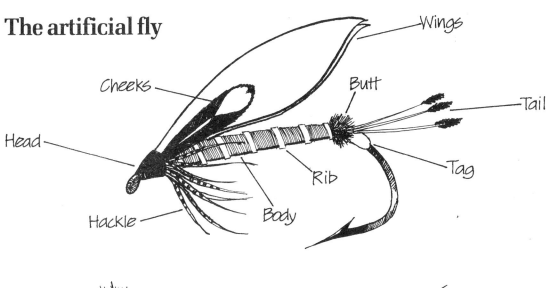

DRY FLIES

Used when fish are taking insects from the surface. Equally effective on river and lake. Most dry flies are tied with the purpose of imitating, as closely as possible, a particular species of insect.

WET FLIES

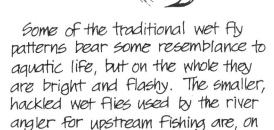

Some of the traditional wet fly patterns bear some resemblance to aquatic life, but on the whole they are bright and flashy. The smaller, hackled wet flies used by the river angler for upstream fishing are, on the other hand, most life-like.

LURES

Lures probably account for more stillwater trout than all the other types combined, mainly because of their more widespread use. Colours used in their construction are as varied as the spectrum. They represent small fish rather than aquatic insect life.

NYMPHS

Mostly fished in conjunction with a floating line. Some patterns are weighted by the inclusion of lead wire beneath the body material. Of all the artificials these are the most life-like. Patterns vary from the very small buzzer pupae up to the large dragonfly nymphs.

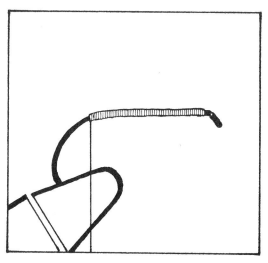

Dubbing a body

Materials for dubbing a body include mole fur, rabbit and hare fur, seal's fur, as well as synthetic fibres in various colours.

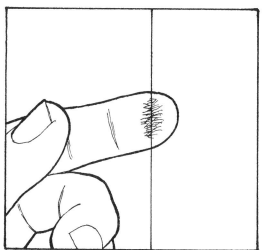

Wind a layer of well waxed silk along the shank of the hook. Apply a further rubbing of wax to the silk hanging between the hook and the bobbin.

Pinch out a very small amount of the required material, between finger and thumb, and place it against the silk. Pinch the material using an even pressure and rotate the dubbing and silk in one direction only. Release finger pressure and repeat the process until the dubbing is left hanging on the silk.

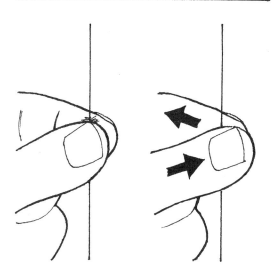
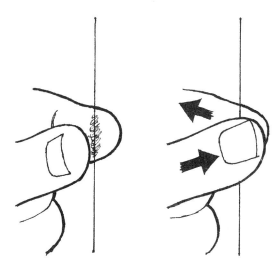

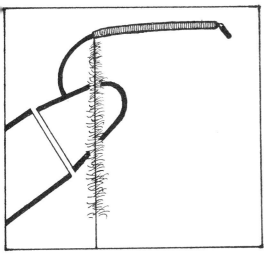

Further spinnings will eventually result in a length of dubbed silk which can be wound up the shank of the hook.

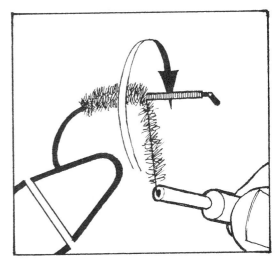

When the required length of dubbing has been wound on to the shank, any excess material left on the hanging silk can be pulled away. The rest of the fly can then be completed in the normal manner.

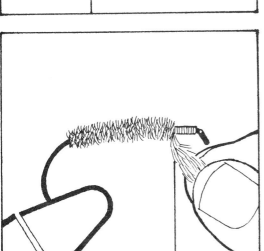

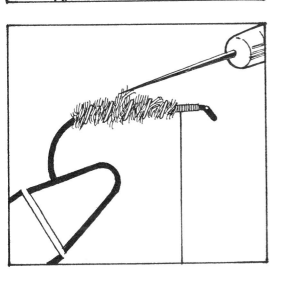

Where a rib material features in a dressing, which it does in most cases, the dubbing tends to flatten a little as the rib is wound over it. The dubbing can be revived by teasing the strands with a dubbing needle.

Making a whip finish (by hand)

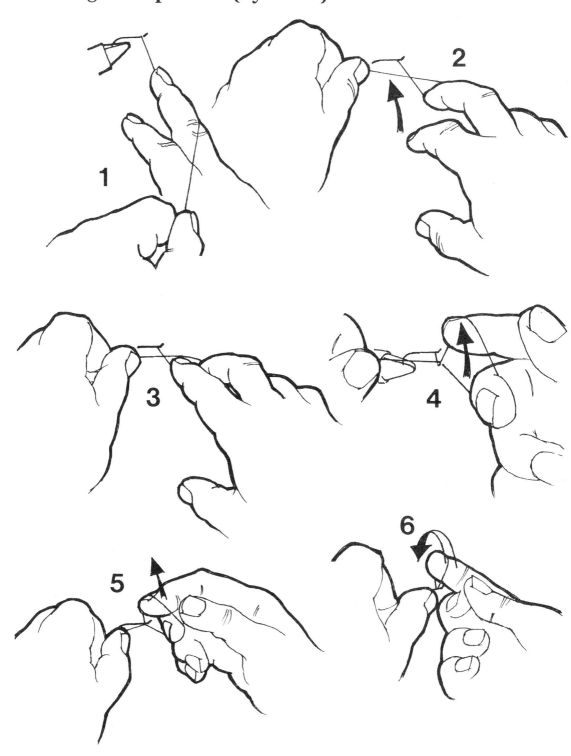

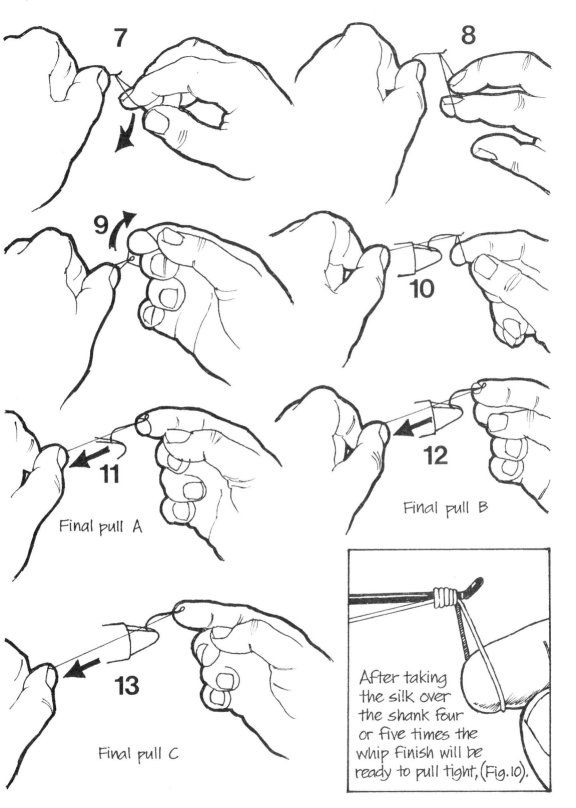

7

8

9

10

11

Final pull A

12

Final pull B

13

Final pull C

After taking
the silk over
the shank four
or five times the
whip finish will be
ready to pull tight, (Fig.10).

Making a whip finish (with a tool)

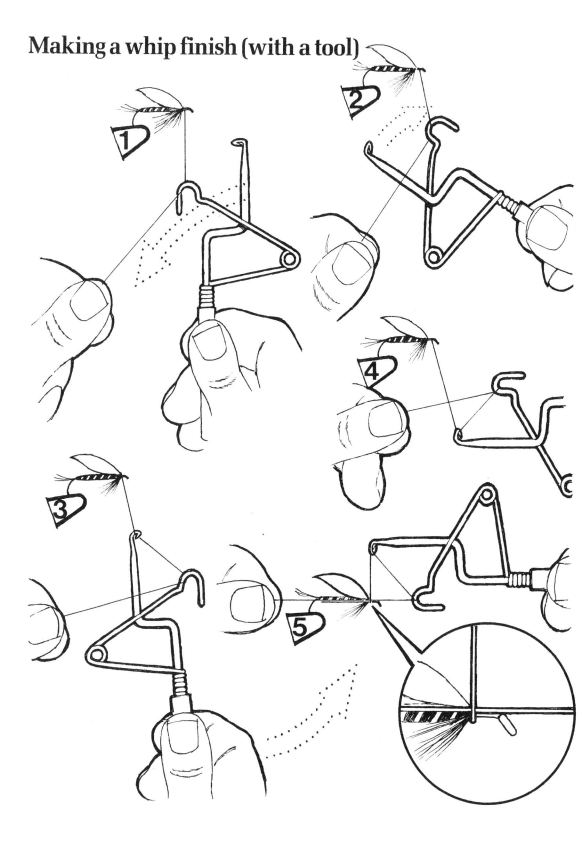

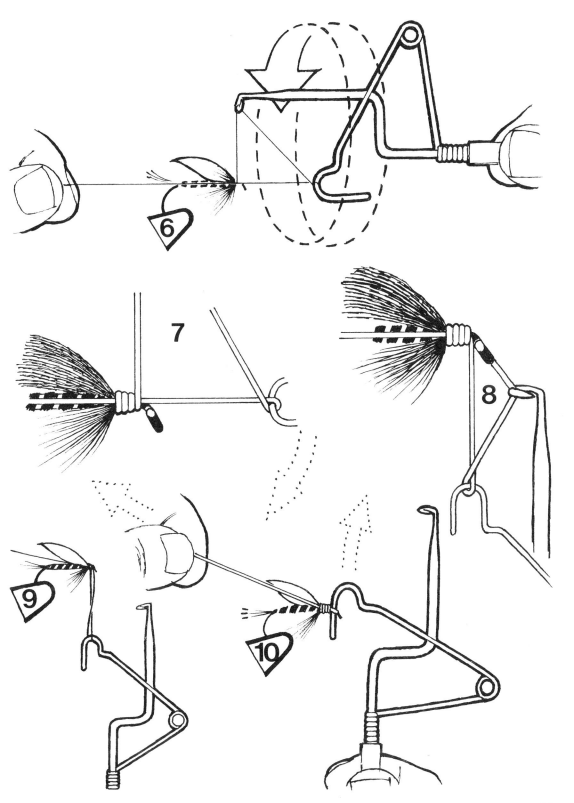

Tying a hackled dry fly

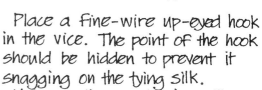

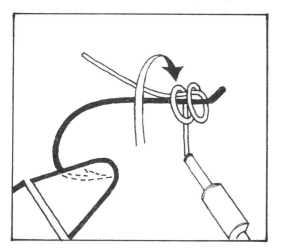

Place a fine-wire up-eyed hook in the vice. The point of the hook should be hidden to prevent it snagging on the tying silk.

Using well-waxed tying silk, wind a neat layer along the shank of the hook. The leading end can be trapped, as shown, and the tag trimmed off before proceeding.

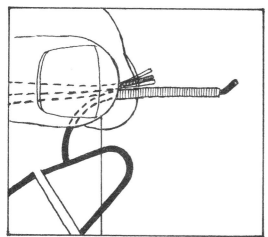

Select a few fibres from a cock hackle (the longer hackles in the cape are best for tails), and tie them in at the bend.

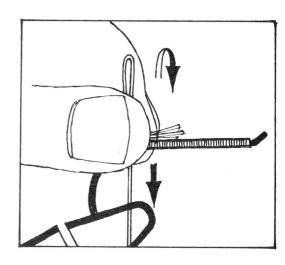

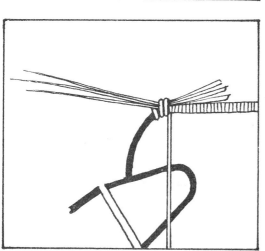

Pinch and loop the silk two or three times over the tail to clamp it to the top of the hook. One turn of silk under the tail will give it a nice cock.

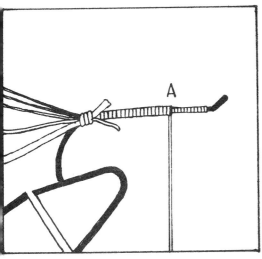

Now trap a length of body material and ribbing. Body materials vary widely, but in this instance we will assume that the fly has a body of floss silk, and a ribbing of gold wire.

After securing the components of the body, wind the silk back to the point where the body is to finish.

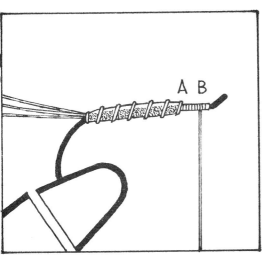

The body floss is now wound on and secured with the tying silk at point 'A'. The ribbing is then wound along the body in neat, even spirals. This also is secured with the tying silk at point 'A'. Excess body and rib material is trimmed off and the tying silk is taken to point 'B'.

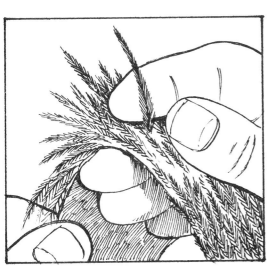

Select a suitable hackle from the cape. This can best be done by bending the cape at the desired spot which will cause the hackles to stand up, making selection a lot easier. The length of the hackle fibre needs to be about one and a half times the gape of the hook.

Tying a hackled dry fly (cont.)

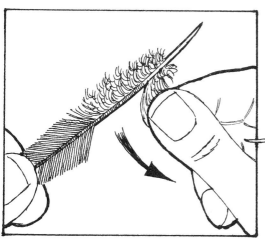

Soft, fluffy fibres near the base of the hackle quill should be pulled off. The prepared hackle should now look like this.

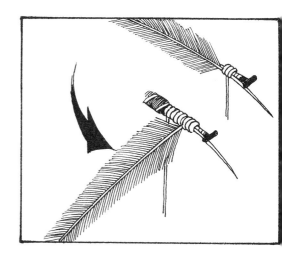

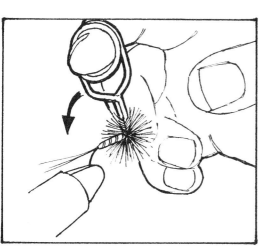

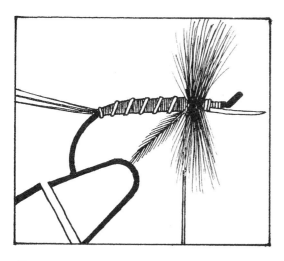

Hold the hackle alongside the hook shank and trap the quill with two or three turns of tying silk, then pull the hackle to a position at right angles to the shank. Continue winding the tying silk, immediately behind the quill, up to the body. The hackle should now be held in a fixed position by tightly butted silk on either side. The concave bias of the hackle should face forwards.

Grip the hackle point with hackle pliers and carefully wind the hackle towards the body, where it should be trapped with two turns of silk.

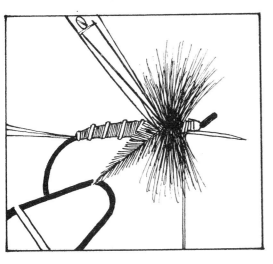

Carefully ease the tying silk back through the hackle, trapping the hackle quill in the process. Snip off the unwanted hackle tip and the excess quill. Trimming with a sharp pair of fly-tying scissors should be done with the utmost care, making sure that the points are clear of the tying silk.

Once the quill has been cut away, the head can be built up and the cut quill-end hidden from view. While this is being done it is best to hold the hackle back, out of the way.

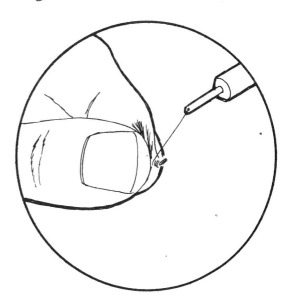

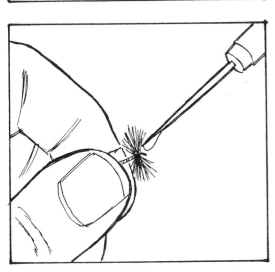

All that remains now is to tie in a whip finish, trim off the tying silk and treat the head of the fly with a drop of clear varnish.

Hackled dry fly dressings

PHEASANT TAIL
Hook   10-14.
Tying silk Brown.
Body   Cock pheasant tail fibres,
         ribbed with gold wire.
Hackle   Golden dun cock.
Tail   Golden dun cock hackle fibres.

COCH-Y-BONDDU
Hook   12-14.
Tying silk Brown.
Body   Two or three strands of
         peacock herl, with fine flat
         gold tinsel tip.
Hackle   Furnace cock.

IRON BLUE DUN
Hook   12-14.
Tying silk Red.
Tail   Iron blue cock hackle fibres.
Body   Mole fur dubbing with a red
         butt.
Hackle   Iron blue cock.

GREY DUSTER
Hook   10-14.
Tying silk Brown.
Body   Dubbing of light rabbit's fur
         mixed with a small amount
         of blue under-fur.
Hackle   Badger cock with a good
         dark centre.

TUP'S INDISPENSABLE
Hook   14-16.
Tying silk Yellow.
Body   Rear end- Yellow floss or
         tying silk. Remainder-
         pinkish lamb's wool.
Hackle   Honey cock.
Tail   Honey cock hackle fibres.

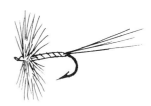

BLUE UPRIGHT
Hook   10-14.
Tying silk, Purple.
Body   Well marked stripped
         peacock quill.
Hackle   Medium blue dun cock.
Tail   Medium blue dun cock fibres.

RED SPINNER

Hook	12-14.
Tying silk	Brown.
Tail	Red cock hackle Fibres.
Body	Red Floss, ribbed with fine Flat gold tinsel.
Hackle	Rear- Red cock.
	Front- Blue dun cock.

GINGER QUILL

Hook	14-16.
Tying silk	Orange.
Tail	Ginger cock hackle Fibres.
Body	Stripped peacock quill.
Hackle	Ginger cock.

MARCH BROWN

Hook	10-14.
Tying silk	Yellow.
Tail	Brown partridge Fibres.
Body	Hare's fur spun thinly.
Hackle	Rear- Dun cock.
	Front- Brown partridge back feather.

RED TAG

Hook	12-14.
Tying silk	Brown.
Tag	Bright red wool or red Floss.
Body	Bronze green peacock herl.
Hackle	Red cock.

CINNAMON QUILL

Hook	12-14.
Tying silk	Brown.
Tail	Ginger cock hackle Fibres.
Body	Stripped peacock herl.
Hackle	Ginger cock.

DOUBLE BADGER

Hook	12-14.
Tying silk	Black.
Body	Three strands of peacock herl.
Hackle	Badger cock - one at the head and one at the tail.

Tying an upright-winged dry fly

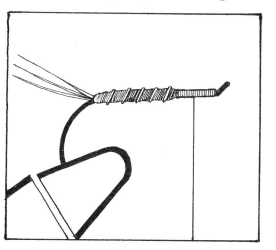

Place a fine-wire hook in the vice and proceed exactly as with a hackled dry fly up to the point where the body has been completed.

It is purely a matter of choice whether an up-eyed or down-eyed hook is used. The former looks prettier, but I doubt very much that the trout has such aesthetic discrimination.

The wings are cut from a pair of matching left and right wing feathers.

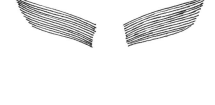

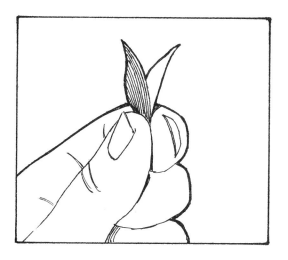

When placed together the wing slips should have the concave faces pointing outwards. Handle the slips very gingerly at this stage, as they have a tendency to break up. If this does occur, cut a new set.

To minimize the risk of this happening grip the slips firmly; try to avoid a sliding movement between finger and thumb.

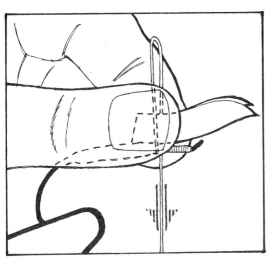

Pinch the slips together between the forefinger and thumb and hold them on the hook shank. Form a long loop over the slips, between finger and thumb, and pull down to trap the wings against the hook shank. Three turns of silk should be enough to hold the slips in place. Check that the slips are sitting squarely along the hook shank.

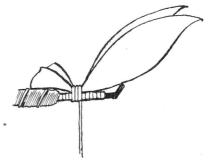

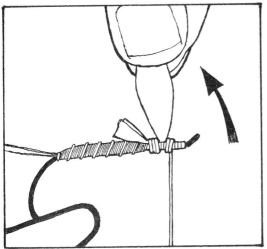

Move the finger and thumb to the tip of the slips and lift them upright. Make a couple of turns of silk tight against the front edge of the slips to trap them in an upright position.

Take one turn of silk around the base of the wing slips.

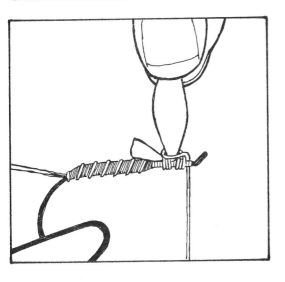

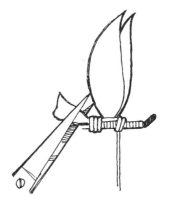

Trim off any excess wing material.

Tying an upright-winged dry fly (cont.)

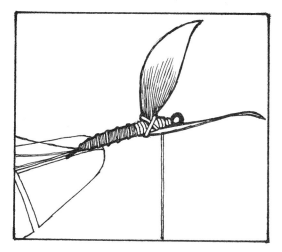

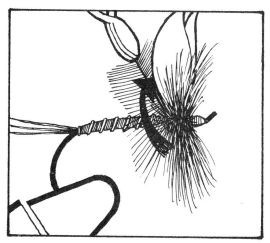

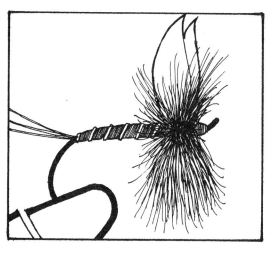

Now make a cross-over of silk between the wings, easing them apart a little more.

Select a good quality cock hackle and tie on, using the same procedure as in the tying of the hackled dry fly. Wind the hackle carefully around the shank, first in front of the wings, then to the rear. Trap the end of the hackle with tying silk and then bring the silk back through the hackle, making sure that the wings are not disfigured in the process.

Trim off the waste hackle point and quill, build up a neat head, whip finish and trim off the silk. Coat the head with clear varnish.

Winged dry fly dressings

COACHMAN
Hook 10-16.
Silk Brown.
Body Bronze peacock herl.
Wings From a white duck wing.
Hackle Natural red cock.

RED QUILL
Hook 14-16.
Silk Red.
Body Stripped peacock herl.
Wings From a starling wing.
Hackle and tail Red cock.

FLIGHT'S FANCY
Hook 12-16.
Silk Yellow.
Body Pale yellow floss, ribbed with flat gold tinsel.
Wings From a pale starling wing.
Hackle and tail Honeydun cock.

POPE'S NONDESCRIPT
Hook 12-16.
Silk Crimson.
Body Apple green floss, ribbed with flat gold tinsel.
Wings From a starling wing.
Hackle and tail Red cock.

HARDY'S FAVOURITE
Hook 10-14.
Silk Red.
Body Claret floss silk, ribbed with bronze peacock herl.
Wings From a woodcock wing.
Hackle Partridge breast feather.
Tail Golden pheasant tippets.

GOLD-RIBBED HARE'S EAR
Hook 12-16.
Silk Yellow.
Body Dubbed hare's fur ribbed with flat gold tinsel.
Wings From a pale wing feather of a starling.
Hackle Longer strands of the body picked out with a needle.

YELLOW SALLY

Hook 12-16.
Silk Primrose.
Body Yellow dyed seal's fur, ribbed with primrose tying silk.
Wings From any fine light-coloured wing dyed yellow.
Hackle Natural light ginger cock.

WICKHAM'S FANCY

Hook 12-14.
Silk Brown.
Body Flat gold tinsel, ribbed with fine gold wire.
Tail Red cock fibres.
Wings From starling or duck wing.
Hackle Red game cock.

ROUGH OLIVE

Hook 12-14.
Silk Brown.
Body Heron herl dyed olive, ribbed with gold wire.
Wings From a starling wing feather.
Hackle Dark blue dun cock.

DRIFFIELD DUN

Hook 14-16.
Silk Yellow.
Body Pale blue seal's fur, ribbed with yellow tying silk.
Wings From a pale starling feather.
Hackle Ginger cock.

GREENWELL'S GLORY

Hook 12-14.
Silk Yellow (well waxed).
Body Yellow tying silk, ribbed with fine gold wire.
Wings From a dark starling feather.
Hackle Light furnace cock.

HOFLAND'S FANCY

Hook 12-16.
Silk Yellow.
Body Crimson floss with yellow tying silk butt.
Wings From a hen pheasant wing.
Hackle Natural red cock.

Tying a variant dry fly

Tie the wings exactly as shown for the upright-wing version, but omit the turns of silk which bring the wings to the upright position as shown in Fig. 6.

Tie the complete hackle to the rear of the wings, then bring the silk to the front of the wings, whip finish and varnish.

BADGER VARIANT

Tying silk	Red.
Body	Stripped peacock quill.
Wings	From a starling wing feather.
Hackle	Badger cock, large.

RED VARIANT

Tying silk	Red.
Body	Stripped peacock quill.
Wings	From a starling wing feather.
Hackle	Natural red cock, large.

RUSTY VARIANT

Tying silk	Red.
Body	Yellow floss.
Wings	From a partridge wing feather.
Hackle	Rusty dun cock, large.

GREENWELL'S VARIANT

Body	Waxed yellow tying silk ribbed with fine gold wire.
Wings	From a starling wing feather.
Hackle	Light furnace cock, large.

Tying a spent-wing dry fly

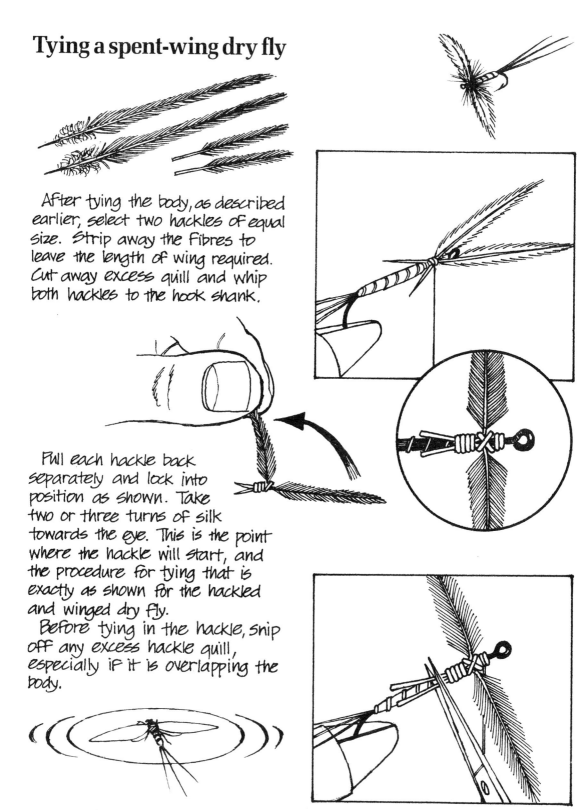

After tying the body, as described earlier, select two hackles of equal size. Strip away the fibres to leave the length of wing required. Cut away excess quill and whip both hackles to the hook shank.

Pull each hackle back separately and lock into position as shown. Take two or three turns of silk towards the eye. This is the point where the hackle will start, and the procedure for tying that is exactly as shown for the hackled and winged dry fly.

Before tying in the hackle, snip off any excess hackle quill, especially if it is overlapping the body.

Spent-wing dry fly dressings

LUNN'S PARTICULAR

Hook	14–16.
Tying silk	Crimson.
Tail	Natural red cock hackle fibres.
Body	Natural red cock hackle stalk.
Wings	Medium blue dun cock hackle tips.
Hackle	Natural medium red cock.

HOUGHTON RUBY

Hook	14–16.
Tying silk	Crimson.
Tail	White cock hackle fibres.
Body	Hackle stalk dyed red.
Wings	Light blue dun hen hackle tips.
Hackle	Bright Rhode Island Red cock.

WINGED YELLOW BOY

Hook	14–16.
Tying silk	Pale orange.
Tail	Pale buff hackle fibres.
Body	White hackle stalk dyed medium yellow.
Wings	Light buff cock hackle tips.
Hackle	Light buff cock.

SHERRY SPINNER

Hook	14–16
Tying silk	Pale orange.
Tail	Pale ginger hackle fibres.
Body	Orange floss silk ribbed with fine gold wire.
Wings	Light blue dun hen hackle tips.
Hackle	Rhode Island Red cock.

Mayfly dressings

SPENT GNAT
Tail	Three fibres from a cock pheasant tail.
Body	White translucent plastic.
Wings	Dark blue hackle points.
Hackle	Badger cock.

YELLOW PARTRIDGE HACKLE
Tail	Three fibres from a cock pheasant tail.
Body	White floss silk.
Rear hackle	Yellow cock.
Front hackle	Grey partridge.

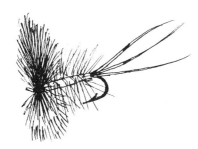

HACKLE FIBRE WING
Tail	Three fibres from a cock pheasant tail.
Body	Natural raffia, ribbed with silver oval tinsel.
Body hackle	Medium olive cock.
Wings	Fibres of large honey dun cock hackle dyed olive, and tied upright.
Shoulder hackle	Badger cock dyed yellow.

HACKLED SPENT
Tail	Three or more fibres from the rump feather of a golden pheasant.
Body	Fluorescent white floss.
Rear hackle	Black cock.
Shoulder hackle	White, grizzle or badger cock.

tying a Hawthorn fly

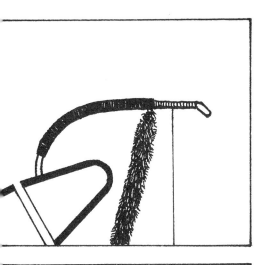

Place a size 10 or 12 down-eyed sproat hook in the vice and run tying silk from the eye to well around the bend. Tie in a length of black floss and take the silk and floss back two-thirds of the way along the shank. At this point, tie in a length of black chenille.

Just forward of the chenille, tie in two white cock hackle points.

Take the silk forward a little and wind the chenille carefully forward, around the wings, to build up a thorax.

Select a very long-fibred cock or hen hackle and tie in immediately forward of the thorax. Pull all the fibres down and trap the bases with tying silk, building up a head in the process. Whip finish and coat the head with black varnish.

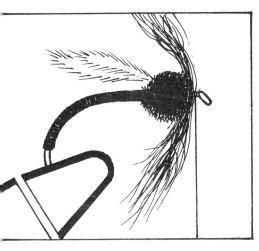

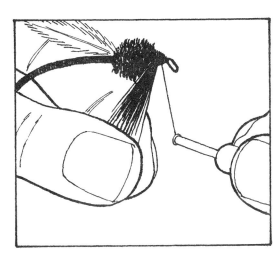

Tying a winged wet fly

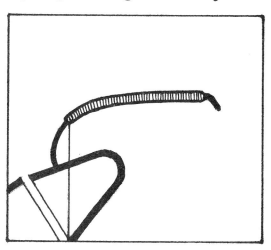

Clamp a down-eyed sproat hook in the vice and run a layer of waxed tying silk along the shank.

The characteristic bend of a sproat hook can be used to good effect by taking the tying silk well into the bend, giving the body a more natural, less rigid appearance

Select the tail material and tie it down with two or three turns of silk. Follow this with a length of ribbing, if required, and finally a length of body material. Return the tying silk back towards the eye, leaving enough space to tie in the hackle and wings.

Wind the body material along the shank and tie it down. Follow this with the rib, which should be evenly spaced along the body.

I usually take a turn of ribbing around the hook shank before proceeding along the body.

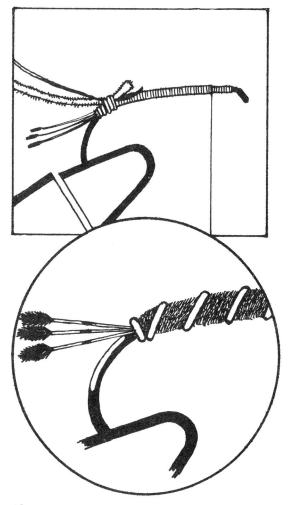

Trim off excess body and ribbing material in preparation for tying in the hackle and wings.

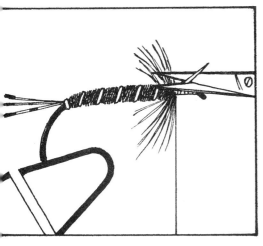

Select a hackle of the type required and tie down with the face of the feather looking forward, so that when it is wound on to the shank the fibres have a bias towards the bend of the hook. Two or three turns of hackle are ample. Tie down the hackle point and cut it away, then return the silk to the front of the hackle and trim off excess quill.

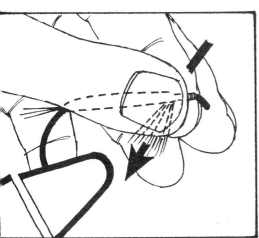

Moisten the forefinger and thumb and brush the hackle down and back. Make two or three turns of silk at the junction of the hackle and hook shank. The result should look like this.

Select two matching slips from a wing feather. Place them together so that the convex edges are facing outwards, opposite to those used on a dry fly.

Tying a winged wet fly (cont.)

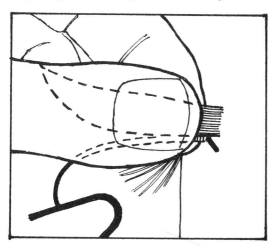

Grip the wing slips firmly between forefinger and thumb and position them on the hook shank. The point of the wings should just overlap the extreme end of the hook bend.

Clamp the wings firmly against the shank of the hook with two or three pinch and loops.

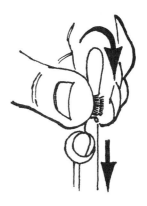

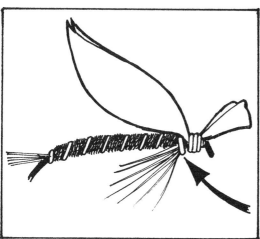

If the wings need to be lifted a little in order to improve the appearance of the fly a turn of tying silk can be taken to the rear.

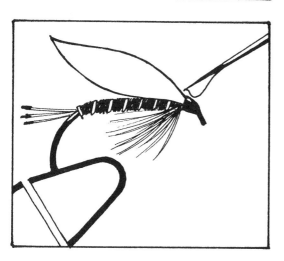

Trim away the excess wing material, build up a stream-lined head and whip finish.

Finally, using the dubbing needle, give the head a coat of varnish.

Winged wet fly dressings

SILVER MARCH BROWN

Tail   Fibres from partridge back feather.
Body   Flat silver tinsel, ribbed oval silver tinsel.
Hackle Partridge back feather.
Wings From hen pheasant wing.

ALEXANDRA

Tail   Red ibis feather slip.
Body   Flat silver tinsel.
Hackle Black hen.
Wings Six to eight strands of green peacock sword herl, with a slip of red ibis each side.

BUTCHER

Tail   Red ibis slip.
Body   Flat silver tinsel.
Hackle Black hen.
Wings From the blue wing-feather of a mallard drake.

ALDER

Body   Peacock herl ribbed with claret tying silk.
Hackle Black hen.
Wings From a brown speckled hen's wing feather.

PETER ROSS

Tail   Fibres from a golden pheasant tippet feather.
Body   Rear half – Flat silver tinsel. Front half – Dyed red seal's fur.
Rib   Oval silver tinsel over both halves.
Hackle Black hen.
Wings From the breast or flank feather of a teal.

MALLARD & CLARET

Tail   Fibres from a golden pheasant tippet feather.
Body   Claret seal's fur.
Rib   Oval gold tinsel.
Hackle Natural red cock.
Wings Bronze speckled feather from a mallard shoulder.

49

CONNEMARA BLACK

Tail   Golden pheasant crest feather.
Body   Black seal's fur, ribbed with fine oval tinsel.
Hackle Natural black cock beneath blue jay fibres.
Wings From the bronze shoulder feather of a mallard.

DUNKELD

Tail   Golden pheasant crest.
Body   Flat gold tinsel, ribbed with oval gold tinsel.
Hackle Dyed orange cock tied palmer fashion.
Wings Bronze mallard.
Cheeks Two jungle cock feathers.

INVICTA

Tail   Golden pheasant crest feather.
Body   Yellow seal's fur, ribbed with oval gold tinsel.
Body hackle Ginger cock.
Head hackle Blue jay fibres.
Wings From a hen pheasant tail feather.

PARMACHENE BELLE

Tail   Red and white duck feather.
Butt   Black ostrich herl.
Body   Yellow floss silk, ribbed with flat gold tinsel.
Hackle Dyed scarlet cock and white cock.
Wings White duck with a red ibis slip each side.

PROFESSOR

Tail   Red ibis feather slip.
Body   Yellow floss silk, ribbed with gold tinsel.
Hackle Natural ginger cock.
Wing   From the flank feather of a grey mallard.

ROYAL COACHMAN

Tail   Strands from a golden pheasant tippet.
Body   Scarlet floss with a bronze peacock herl butt and thorax.
Hackle Natural light red cock.
Wings Slips from any white wing feather.

Tying a Corixa (Water-boatman)

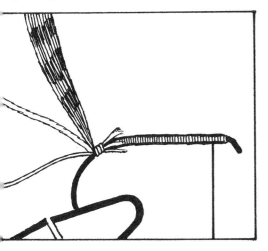

Clamp a size 12-14 down-eyed hook in the vice and run tying silk to the bend. Tie in a length of wire or oval tinsel ribbing, followed by a length of green or orange wool. Take a slip of fibres from a cock pheasant tail feather and tie at the same point, then run the silk back, almost to the eye.

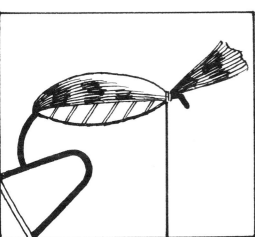

Build up a body with the wool and tie it down. Run the ribbing in neat spirals back along the body and tie it down. Trim off excess body and rib material.

Now pull the pheasant fibres right over the body, tie down and trim away excess material.

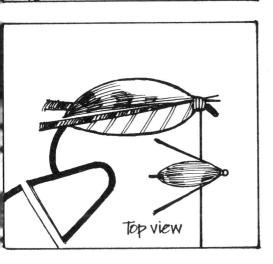

Top view

Select two long fibres from a cock pheasant tail and tie on at each side of the head. The thicker ends of the fibres should point to the rear. Build up a large head and treat it with a coat of clear varnish. A layer of clear varnish over the back is also advisable.

Tying a hackled wet fly

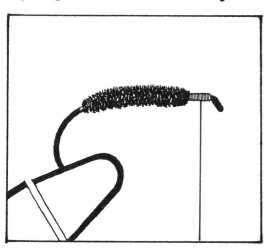

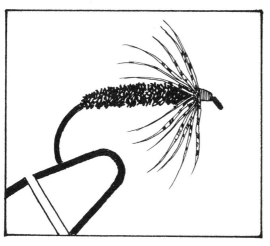

Hackles used for this type of fly need to be soft. Partridge, hen, snipe or woodcock are ideal.

When fished in running water the fibres of these hackles move in the current, giving the fly a most life like appearance.

Place a down-eyed size 14-10 hook in the vice and tie in a body.

Select a good quality hackle and tether it to the hook shank with the face of the feather pointing forward. Hold the tip of the hackle with hackle pliers and make just two or three turns around the shank.

Trim off excess hackle tip and quill, build up a neat head and coat it with clear varnish.

Hackle before preparation

Hackle ready to be tied

Hackled wet fly dressings

PARTRIDGE & ORANGE
Body Bright orange floss or silk.
Hackle Brown partridge back feather.

BROWN SPIDER
Body Bronze peacock herl.
Hackle Brown partridge back feather.

SNIPE & PURPLE
Body Purple floss.
Hackle Small feather from snipe's wing.

BRACKEN CLOCK
Body Bronze peacock herl and red silk.
Hackle Cock pheasant neck feather.

BLACK SPIDER
Body Black tying silk or floss.
Hackle Black hen hackle.

WATERHEN BLOA
Body Mole fur spun on yellow silk.
Hackle Feather from underside of moorhen's wing.

BLACK & PEACOCK SPIDER
Body Three strands of peacock herl over black floss underbody.
Hackle Black hen hackle.

GROUSE & YELLOW
Body Yellow floss silk ribbed with fine gold wire.
Hackle Grouse breast feather.

Tying a palmer

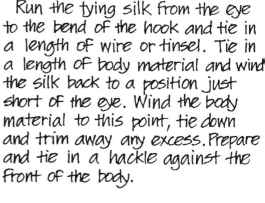

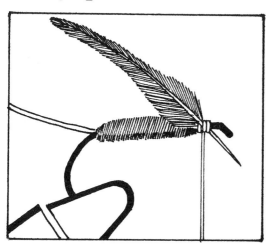

Run the tying silk from the eye to the bend of the hook and tie in a length of wire or tinsel. Tie in a length of body material and wind the silk back to a position just short of the eye. Wind the body material to this point, tie down and trim away any excess. Prepare and tie in a hackle against the front of the body.

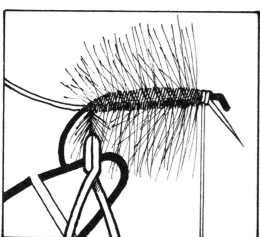

Grip the hackle point in a pair of hackle pliers and take the hackle, around the body, to the bend of the hook. Now, very carefully but firmly, wind the ribbing back through the hackle and tie it down with the silk. The ribbing is now holding the hackle stem secure all along the body.

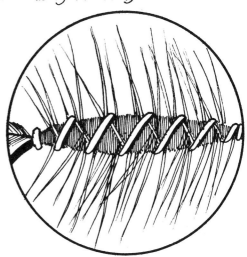

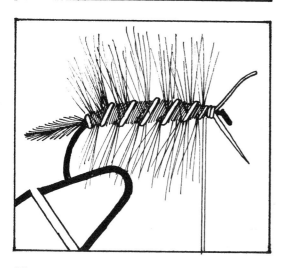

Remove the hackle pliers and trim away the hackle point, excess quill and ribbing material.

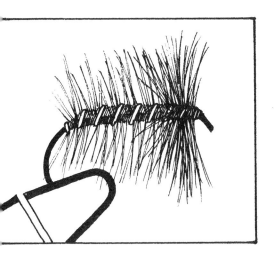

An extra hackle can now be tied at the front, if required. In my opinion this improves the appearance of the fly and helps to provide extra buoyancy if it is being used as a floating pattern.

On predominantly dark patterns a white forward hackle aids visibility when the fly is being fished in shadow beneath overhanging foliage.

Palmer dressings

BROWN PALMER
Body   Brown wool or seal's fur.
Rib   Gold wire or oval gold tinsel.
Hackle Brown cock.

STEEL BLUE
Body   Peacock herl with orange tag.
Rib   Gold wire.
Hackle Grizzle cock.

ZULU
Tail   Red ibis feather or red wool.
Body   Black wool or seal's fur.
Rib   Flat silver tinsel.
Hackle Black cock.

ARTFUL DODGER
Body   Purple wool.
Rib   Gold wire.
Wings   From a cock pheasant's wing.
Hackle Red cock.

Tying a nymph

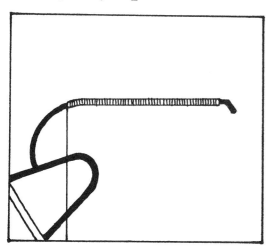

Place a long-shanked hook in the vice and run tying silk from the eye to the bend.

Tie in the tail material, if needed, followed by the ribbing and the body material.

In this instance we will assume that the body is made of seal's fur, which has to be dubbed on to the tying silk prior to being wound along the hook shank.(see section on dubbing a body).

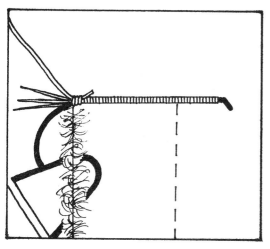

Take the dubbed silk, in turns, about two-thirds of the way back along the hook shank. Remove any excess dubbing from the hanging silk. Now carefully wind the rib material along the body and tie it down. A slip of feather fibres is now tied in by one end, which eventually forms the wing cases.

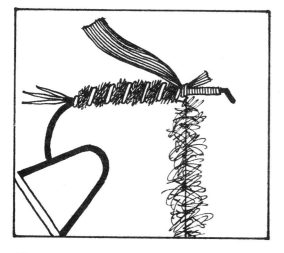

More seal's fur is now dubbed on to the silk in preparation for forming the thorax. This is usually a different colour to the main body. Remember not to overdo the dubbing as this will result in a bulky mess.

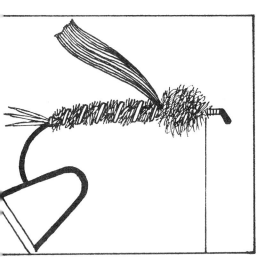

Wind the dubbed silk towards the eye of the hook. Stop just short of the eye, leaving enough space to tie in the hackle and form the head.

The hackle is tied in exactly the same way as that of a hackled wet fly. Trim away any excess hackle quill.

Now grip the end of the feather fibres and pull them over the thorax and the hackle. Tie down with a few turns of silk and trim away any excess material. Build a neat head, whip finish, trim off silk and varnish.

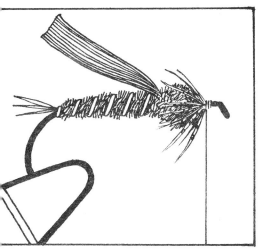

Some patterns of nymph have wing cases over the body or over the body and thorax.

Wing cases tied in at the bend of the hook and pulled over before the thorax is dubbed.

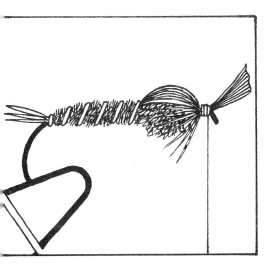

Wing cases tied in at the bend of the hook and pulled over before the head is formed.

Nymph dressings

SEDGE PUPA (JOHN GODDARD)
Body   Orange seal's fur.
Rib   Oval silver tinsel.
Thorax   Dark brown condor herl.
Wing cases Pale brown condor herl.
Hackle   Honey hen, tied sparsely.

MAYFLY NYMPH
Tail   Three strands from a cock
            pheasant's tail feather.
Body   Natural seal's fur.
Thorax   Brown olive seal's fur.
Rib   Oval gold tinsel.
Wing cases From a hen pheasant tail.
Hackle   Brown partridge.

AMBER NYMPH
Body   Amber yellow seal's fur.
Thorax   Dark brown or orange
            seal's fur.
Wing cases Fibres of any brownish
            feather tied over the body.
Hackle   Honey hen hackle fibres.

PAMSELFLY NYMPH
Tail   Three olive green hackle
            points.
Body   Olive seal's fur.
Rib   Flat gold tinsel.
Thorax   Dark olive seal's fur.
Wing cases Fibres from a brown
            mallard shoulder feather.
Hackle   Grouse hackle fibres.

MONTANA STONE
Body   Black chenille.
Thorax   Yellow or orange chenille.
Wing cases Black chenille.
Hackle   Black hen.

IVEN'S GREEN & BROWN NYMPH
Tail   Three strands of peacock herl.
Body   Olive green ostrich herl.
Wing cases Peacock herl.
Thorax   Peacock herl.

Tying a Midge Pupa (Buzzer)

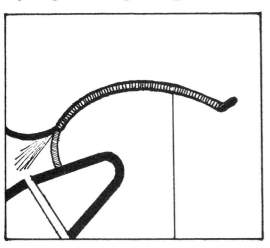

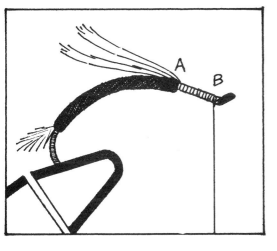

There are many variations on this imitation and, no doubt, they all take their share of trout if fished correctly. My variation is no exception and is simplicity itself to tie.

Place a size 16–10 Yorkshire caddis hook in the vice and run well waxed tying silk from the eye to well around the bend. Tie in a plume made from a short length of fluorescent white floss. A tap with the finger on the end of the floss will open it out.

Tie in a length of brown, black or green floss and take the tying silk back to point A. Wind on the floss body and tie down.

Tie in two or three lengths of fluorescent white floss and wind the silk to point B. Wind the strands of white floss, together, to point B, and tie down. Whip finish and varnish.

The plume at the front may have to be trimmed, and a few taps with the finger will open out the fibres to give a natural appearance.

Tying a lure (hackle-winged)

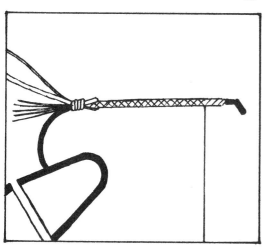

Clamp a down-eyed long-shanked hook in the vice and run well-waxed silk, in open turns, up to the bend. Tie in the tail, if needed followed by the ribbing and the body material and run the silk back just short of the eye.

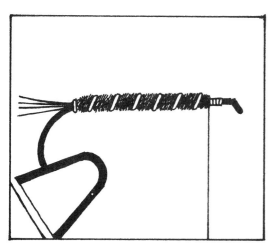

Wind the body material back to the hanging silk and tie it down. Do the same with the rib, making sure that it is evenly spaced all the way along the body. Trim off excess material.

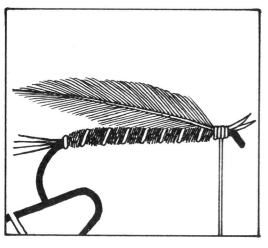

Select two long, good quality cock hackles and hold them, back-to-back, between forefinger and thumb along the top of the body. The hackle points should extend just beyond the bend of the hook. Using the pinch and loop method, tie them down with three or four turns of silk.

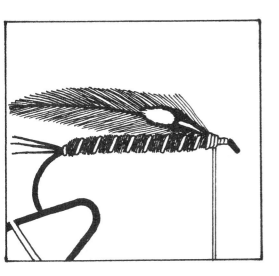

Owing to their scarcity and price jungle cock feathers are not used as often as they once were. However, there are signs that they will once again be readily available in the not-too-distant future, as the bird is being reared in captivity by a few enterprising and imaginative breeders. If you do possess any of these striking feathers now is the point at which to tie them in, on each side of the wings. Check to see that they are positioned nicely before proceeding any further.

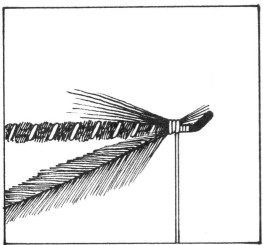

Turn the hook over in the vice. Pull off a bunch of fibres from a cock hackle, and using the pinch and loop method secure them with two or three turns of silk. Before tying them down completely, rub across the fibres with the thumb nail to spread them a little.

Build up a sleek-looking head and whip finish. Coat the head with red or black varnish. An eye decoration can be painted on if jungle cock is not being used.

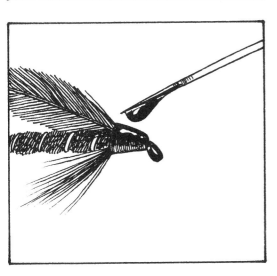

Tying a lure (hair-winged)

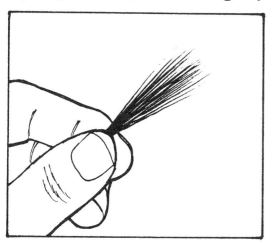

Place a long-shanked down-eyed hook in the vice and run well-waxed tying silk down to the bend. Using the required materials, make the body in the usual manner.

Cut a bunch of hairs of the required variety and lay it along the top of the hook shank. The tips of the hairs should extend just beyond the bend of the hook.

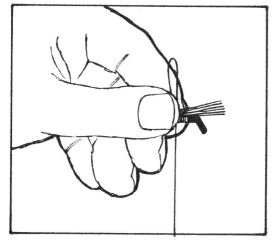

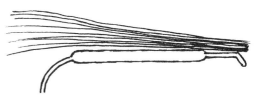

Take three or four turns of silk around the hairs and hook-shank using the pinch-and-loop procedure.

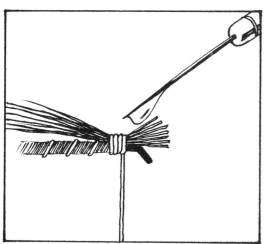

Half hitch

To prevent the fibres coming adrift during use, apply a blob of clear varnish which will be sucked into the wing by the capillary action of the hairs. Take a few more turns of silk around the hairs and make a half hitch.

Turn the fly over in the vice and tie on a beard hackle in exactly the same way as for the hackle-winged lure, and trim off any excess hackle.

Turn the fly upright again and trim off any excess wing material.

When trimming off excess wing material, cut at an angle, in order to produce a neater head.

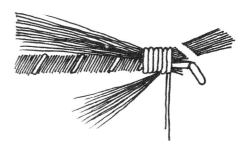

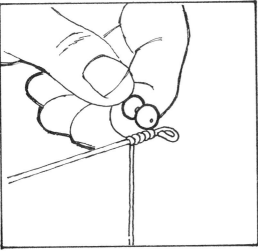

An additional embellishment for hackle or hairwing lures can be made by cutting a section of ball chain and tying this, in the manner shown, to produce a bug-eyed look.

Dressing omitted for the sake of clarity.

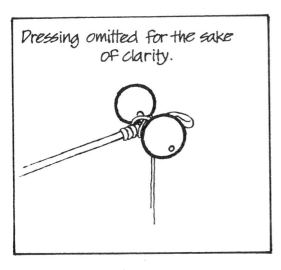

Lure dressings

MISSIONARY

Tail   Scarlet-dyed cock hackle
      Fibres.
Body   White chenille.
Rib   Silver tinsel.
Wing   Whole mallard breast feather.
Hackle Scarlet-dyed cock hackle
      Fibres.

JERSEY HERD

Tail and Back Fibres of bronze
      peacock herl.
Body   Shaped with silk and covered
      with gold tinsel.
Hackle Hot orange cock.
Head   Two or three turns of
      peacock herl.

BADGER LURE

Body   Fluorescent orange wool.
Rib   Oval silver tinsel.
Wing   Two large badger cock hackles.
Hackle Hot orange cock hackle fibres.
Eyes   Two jungle cock feathers.

VIVA

Tag   Lime green fluorescent wool.
Body   Black chenille.
Rib   Flat silver tinsel.
Wing   Black marabou fibres.
Hackle Black cock hackle fibres.

ACE OF SPADES

Body   Black chenille.
Rib   Oval silver tinsel.
Wing   Black hen hackle tied
      matuka fashion.
Overwing   Bronze mallard.
Hackle   Guinea fowl fibres.

RED & BLACK MATUKA

Body   Red chenille.
Rib   Oval gold tinsel.
Wing   Two black hen hackles tied
      matuka fashion.
Eyes   Jungle cock feathers.
Hackle Black cock hackle fibres.

SWEENEY TODD
Body   Rear – Black floss silk.
       Front – DFM magenta floss.
Rib   Silver tinsel or Lurex.
Hackle Crimson cock.
Wing Black squirrel tail hair.

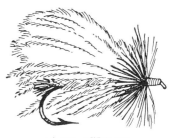

JACK FROST
Tag   Crimson wool.
Body   White wool.
Hackles Crimson cock followed by
        white cock.
Wing   White marabou.

CHURCH FRY
Tail   Bunch of white hackle fibres.
Body   Orange chenille.
Rib   Gold or silver tinsel.
Hackle Crimson.
Wing   Natural grey squirrel tail hair.

BLACK LURE
(Often tied tandem fashion)
Body   Black chenille or floss.
Rib   Silver tinsel.
Hackle Black cock fibres.
Wing   Four black cock hackles.

WHISKY FLY
Silk   Orange
Tag   DFM scarlet nylon floss.
Body   Wide silver tinsel or Lurex.
Rib   DFM scarlet nylon floss.
Hackle Hot orange cock.
Wing   Hot orange calf's tail hair.

BLACK GHOST
Tail   Golden pheasant crest.
Body   Black wool or floss.
Rib   Flat silver tinsel.
Hackle Golden pheasant crest.
Wing   White cock hackles.
Cheeks Jungle cock.

Tying a tandem lure

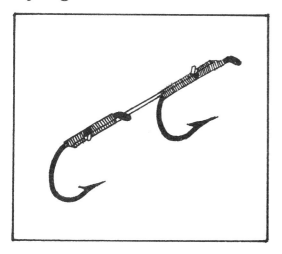

Tandem lures can be tied on long-shank or standard hooks. Cut a length of heavy nylon monofilament line and whip it to two hooks with heavy tying silk. Form a couple of simple hitch knots on the nylon line to prevent it slipping under the whipping. Reinforce this with a coat of clear varnish and allow to dry.

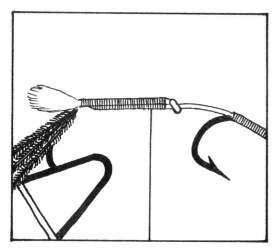

The example shown here is a worm fly, a long-established lure with many large trout to its credit.

Put the rear hook in the vice first and run the tying silk to the bend of the hook. Tie in a tail of red wool and a few fibres of peacock herl. Take the tying silk back, almost to the eye, and wind the body material to the same point and tie it down with silk.

Trim off any excess body herl and tie in a natural dark red hen or cock hackle to slope well back over the body. Whip finish and coat the head with black varnish.

The front hook is then put in the vice and tied in exactly the same manner as the rear hook. The tail, however, is omitted.

Long-shank hook tandem lures have only the body material tied to the rear hook.

Tandem lure dressings

BADGER LURE

Silk	Orange.
Bodies	Fluorescent orange wool.
Rib	Oval silver tinsel.
Hackle	Hot orange cock.
Wing	Two large badger hackles.
Eyes	Two jungle cock feathers.

BLACK LURE

Silk	Black.
Bodies	Black floss or chenille.
Rib	Oval silver tinsel.
Hackle	Black cock fibres.
Wing	Two or four long, black cock hackles.

SWEENEY TODD TANDEM

Silk	Black.
Bodies	Black floss silk.
Rib	Oval silver tinsel.
Throat	Magenta fluorescent wool.
Hackle	Crimson cock hackle fibres.
Wing	Black squirrel tail fibres.

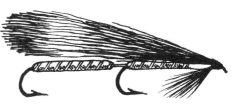

CHURCH FRY TANDEM

Silk	Brown.
Bodies	Orange floss silk.
Rib	Flat silver tinsel or Lurex.
Throat	Magenta fluorescent wool.
Hackle	Orange cock hackle fibres.
Wing	Grey squirrel tail fibres.

Tying a Muddler Minnow

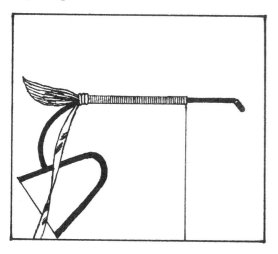

Wind black or brown tying silk from a point half way along the shank of a long-shanked hook to the bend. Tie in a slip of turkey wing for the tail and a length of flat gold tinsel, then return the silk to its starting point. Wind the gold tinsel to form a body, and tie it down.

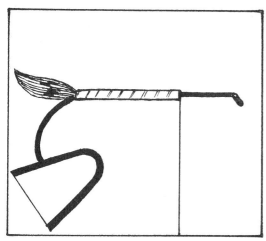

A bunch of grey squirrel tail hair is then tied to the shank to extend well beyond the bend of the hook.

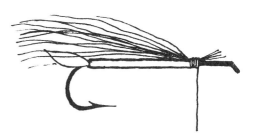

Two sections of mottled (oak) turkey feather are then tied over the squirrel hair, again extending past the bend of the hook. Make a half-hitch at this point in preparation for spinning the deer hair along the bare hook shank.

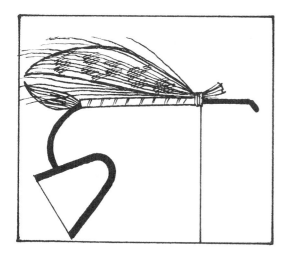

Cut a bunch of deer hair and grip it tightly to prevent the hairs sliding out of place.

Hold the hairs along the top of the hook shank with the cut ends pointing forward.

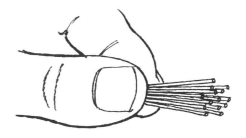

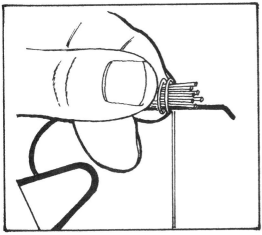

Take two loose turns of silk over the hairs.

Pull down tight on the silk, and at the same time rotate the finger and thumb in the same direction as the turning deer hair. The first spinning should look like this.

Take the silk to the front of the hairs and form a hitch, in readiness for the next spinning.

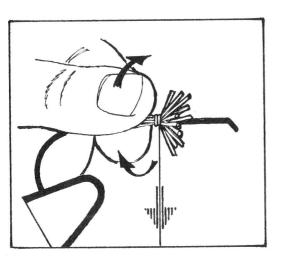

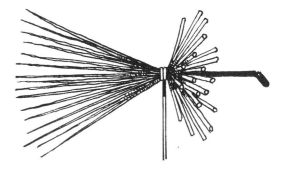

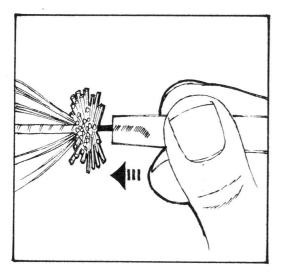

After each spinning the hairs will have to be pushed back. This is best done with an empty ball pen casing or something similar.

After a few spinnings the head will begin to take on a very bushy appearance. Hairs on the forward part of the head need not be full length as the head will have to be trimmed eventually. The drawing below shows how to obtain two spinnings from one length of hairs.

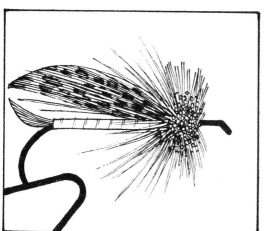

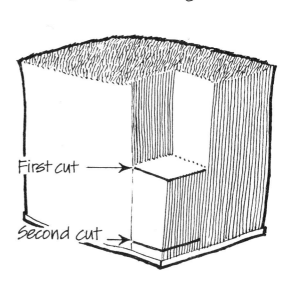

First cut →

Second cut →

Spin the deer hair up to the eye, whip finish and varnish.

Very carefully start to trim the deer hair using sharp fly-tying scissors. The hair points forming the first spinning can be left to slope back over the body.

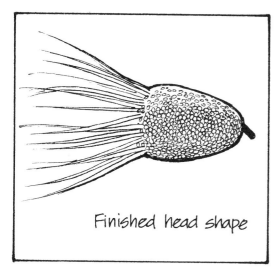

Finished head shape

Tying a Jersey Herd

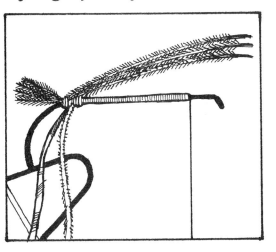

Place a long-shank Nº 6-10 hook in the vice and run the tying silk down to the bend. Tie in a length of wool, flat gold tinsel and a bunch of peacock herl.

Take the silk back to a point short of the eye. Wind the wool towards the hanging silk, building up a cigar-shaped body in the process. Tie down the wool and trim off any excess. The gold tinsel is now wound over the wool body, tied down and trimmed.

Select a hot orange cock hackle and wind on in front of the body.

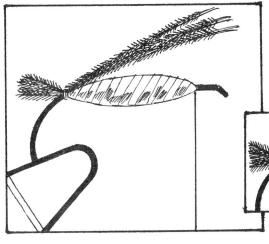

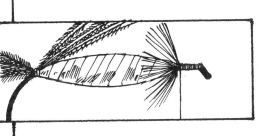

Bring the peacock herls over the body and hackle and tie them down, but do not trim away the excess herl.

Take the tying silk close to the eye and wind the excess herl around the shank to form a head.

Finish off in the usual manner.

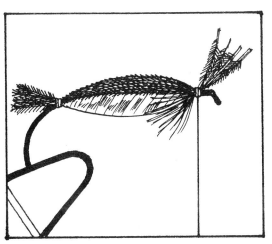

Tying a Matuka lure

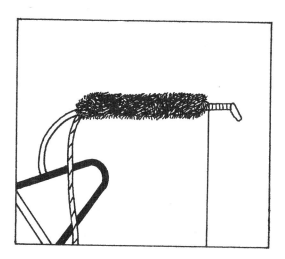

Place a long-shanked Nº 6–10 hook in the vice. Build up a body, which in most matuka patterns is made of chenille, and leave the rib (oval tinsel) hanging, ready for use.

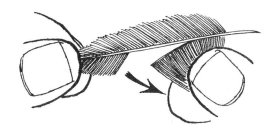

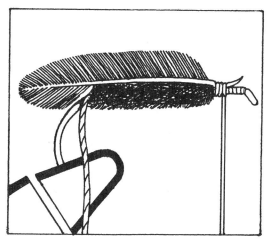

Select a large hen hackle and pull most of the fibres off on one side of the quill.

Place the prepared hackle on top of the body to see if it fits — the hackle should extend over the hook bend by about one-third of the body length. Take two or three turns of silk around the base of the quill to trap the hackle in position.

Very carefully start to wind the rib back through the hackle, adjusting the hackle fibres in the process. Tie down the rib, turn the fly over and tie in a beard hackle. Build up a head with the tying silk, whip finish and coat with black varnish.

Tying a Dog Nobbler

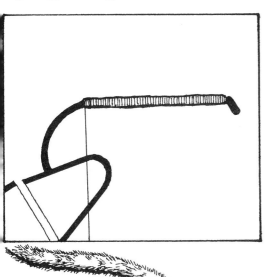

Put a long-shanked hook in the vice and take the tying silk to the bend of the hook.

Select a generous bunch of fibres from a marabou plume and tie in. Cut a length of chenille, tie it down next to the marabou and run the silk back to a point about 5mm short of the eye.

Wind the chenille along the hook shank to form a body, and tie down. Trim off any excess chenille and form a whip finish.

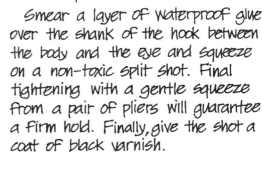

Smear a layer of waterproof glue over the shank of the hook between the body and the eye and squeeze on a non-toxic split shot. Final tightening with a gentle squeeze from a pair of pliers will guarantee a firm hold. Finally, give the shot a coat of black varnish.

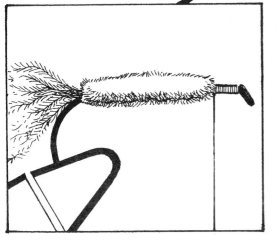

Tying a Shrimp

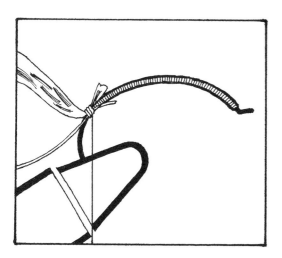

A curved-shank hook will be required to tie this very effective imitation. The 'caddis' hooks made by Partridge are ideal in sizes 16-10.

Take the silk from the eye to a point well around the bend and tie in a length of oval gold tinsel and a length of raffine or clear polythene.

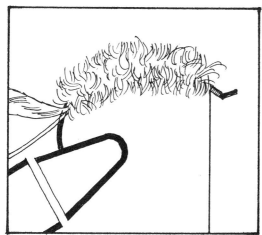

Wax the hanging tying silk and dub with seal's fur. Use a mixture of 90% cream or pale orange and 10% fluorescent red. Wind the dubbed silk to a point just short of the eye.

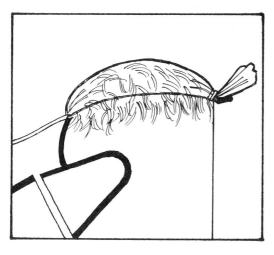

Pull the raffine or polythene completely over the top of the body, and tie it down.

If raffine is being used it must be dampened before doing this.

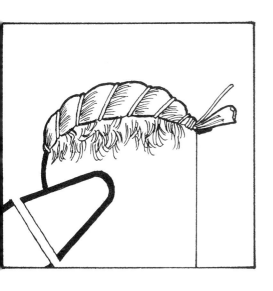

Now bring the ribbing, in neat spirals, over and along the body, and tie it down. Trim off the excess body shell material and ribbing and build up a neat head. Whip Finish, and apply a coat of clear varnish over the head and shell back.

Tying silk colours for this pattern can be cream, orange, yellow or red.

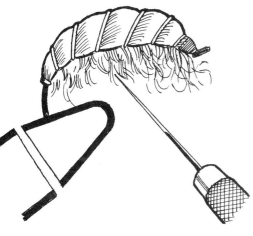

Using a dubbing needle, tease out strands of the body material to give a more life-like appearance.

This pattern can be tied to a standard-shank sproat hook, but in so doing ensure that the curved body shape is retained, by taking the dressing well around the hook bend.

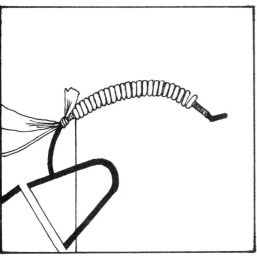

As this little creation is best fished well down in the water it is a good policy to add weight by running a length of lead wire along the shank of the hook before winding on the body.

Tying a Daddy-long-legs

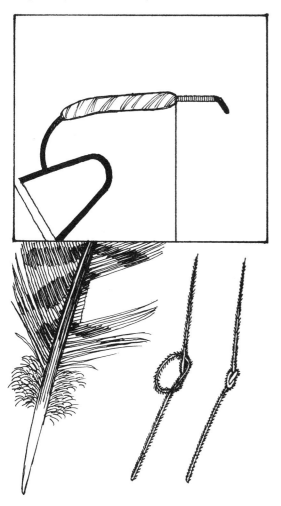

Clamp a long-shanked size 10 hook in the vice and run well-waxed tying silk from the eye to the bend. Tie in a length of raffia or raffine and bring the silk back about two-thirds of the way along the shank. Follow this with the body material, tie down and trim away any excess.

Cut a slip of fibres from a cock pheasant tail feather (the longer the better) and, one by one, separate them and tie a simple knot in the middle. Put these aside on a sheet of white paper or foam.

Turn the hook over in the vice. Select at least six fibres, more if you like, and hold them together between finger and thumb. Rotate them a few times to give a bedraggled look and tie them immediately in front of the body.

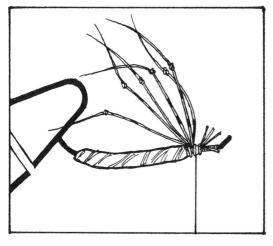

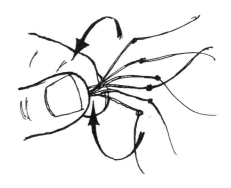

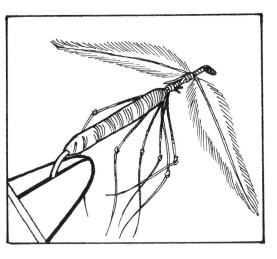

Select two white or honey colour cock hackles and prepare them as you would for tying a spent dry fly. Whip them to the hook so that they point outwards and slightly back.

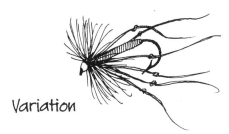

Variation

The hackle is then tied, using a natural red cock hackle, in exactly the same way as the hackle on a spent dry fly. Form a whip finish and coat the head with clear varnish.

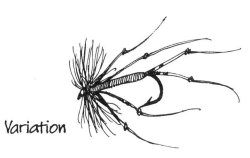

Variation

Tying a sedge (caddis) fly

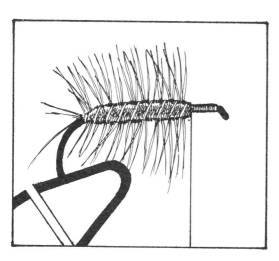

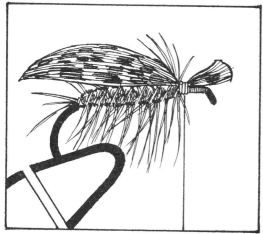

This is another pattern with many variations. Species of the natural insect are numerous and vary in size from the huge great red sedge or murragh, to the smaller sedges, such as silverhorns and yellow sedge.

A good impressionistic pattern can be made by tying a palmered body, as described earlier.

After the body is complete lay a matching pair of wing slips, taken from a mottled turkey tail feather or a hen pheasant wing feather, over the hackle, and tie down to lie low along the body. Immediately in front of the wings, tie in a good quality cock hackle.

This type of dressing provides enough buoyancy, when treated with floatant, to be dragged across the water surface, giving a life-like, scuttling impression of the natural insect.

Storing materials

Fly-tying materials should be stored in a case or cabinet. Portable cases are available on the market, at a reasonable cost. A cabinet, however, will probably have to be specially made. My cabinet is a mahogany creation and was made during the Georgian period. Whether it was originally intended to hold fly-tying materials I do not know, but it certainly does the job well, and is a pleasure to use.

Furs, feathers and floss suffer the depredations of moths if precautions are not taken. A small container housing a napthalene ball will keep these pests away.

Portable fly-tying case

Cabinet

Napthalene container